PASSIVE INCOME

HOW TO MAKE MONEY
WHILE YOU ARE SLEEPING

Passive income  Generating junkie ™

BRANDON K. GATES

Passive Income Generating Junkie

~By: Brandon K. Gates~

TABLE OF CONTENTS

CHAPTER ONE

What Is Passive Income?

With almost everybody tired of working nine-to-five or shifts, passive income has become a popular option for many. The term has been defined differently by various sources. This, in turn, leads to confusion as many people don't seem to understand what this type of income is in reality.

There are people who mistake passive income for income generated without any exerted effort. While this may be true in the later stages, it is not applicable to the earlier stages. And this is why.

An income that is passive may be attained when you are generating income without directly getting involved with the day-to-day work.

So that even when you are not working on your venture for eight hours, the income is still being generated for you.

However, this does not mean that you can generate income without doing anything at all. In reality, you need to do the real job yourself during the early stages. You must first set the "wheels in motion".

So you may ask, **what is passive income?**

Here are the things you should know.

The money you earn without spending large amounts of time are known as passive income. For some, it comes in the form of investments, for others it comes through royalties.

What this means is that you initially invest time and money on a business.

When the business is up and running, it will generate income for you even when you no longer spend much time on it. In other words, create a system, let it work for you, generate income from the system, and find the road to your financial freedom.

This is how you let money work for you instead of you working for money. Stop just trading time for dollars.

What is passive income? It is the income generated when you work hard and plant the seeds now and earn residuals from it later on.

One of the most popular ways to do that is to build a business, implement the system, Pay employees to run the business, and keep the profit.

While some people own the business from the start, others start small and expand later on as the income increases. By the time the business expands, you then literally let the money work for you even when you go to sleep.

After defining what passive income is, it is also important to note what it **IS NOT**. For a clearer understanding, here are some examples.

Side jobs that generate side income are not the same as passive income. Let's say you are maintaining a blog site and earning from it. You cannot earn passive income from it unless you promote some ads on the page through affiliate marketing.

On the other hand, salary raises are also not considered an income that is passive. While additional income is generated for the same amount of time worked, you still need to work for a period of time for it. A raise is just an increase in the income of an employee. It is therefore not equal to passive income.

Passive income is income earned that you do not have to constantly spend time to earn.

After defining what passive income is and what it is not, you should now have a clearer understanding on which road to take towards your financial freedom. This book is designed to help you reach that road like many others have.

CHAPTER TWO

Getting Started

In the previous chapter, we've looked at what's passive income, some general passive income strategies, and how to find your niche. In this chapter, we're going to look at 10 proven passive income ideas that you can use for yourself, in whatever niche you choose.

These ideas are options, you could use several of these ideas together in one business. You should leverage your audience and visitors to generate as many income streams as possible.

If you provide real value, and people are very satisfied, they will naturally want to buy more things from you. So, prudently give them that opportunity!

1. Sell an eBook or other information product online

Creating an eBook and selling it as a downloadable PDF is a very simple method that anybody can use to build a passive income stream. You just have to create a book, or another resource that is valuable to people in your niche.

This could be a tutorial, or how-to guide, a list of resources, a directory, sample resumes, some cybersecurity security templates, ready-written letters, a collection of reviews or tips — anything that people would find useful enough and be willing to pay for it.

You could even re-package a series of blog posts, and sell them as a book. This is quite a popular strategy, as people are ready to pay for the convenience of having everything in one place for referral.

Maybe you already have some specialist knowledge or skills that other people would like to learn, or you've spent a lot of time finding things out that other people need to know.

If you haven't, if you find out what people need, you could learn it yourself and then produce an eBook about it. Or outsource it and get somebody else to write it for you.

A good way to find eBook ideas is to look at books in your niche on Amazon, and see what people are buying, and also what they are saying in the reviews. This will often give you an idea of the shortcomings in existing books.

Maybe there is something you can do better, or you can focus on a specific aspect that the reviewers highlight as what's missing from the existing books.

An eBook doesn't have to be a great big epic manuscript. Some of the most successful eBooks are of little sizes around 10 to 20 pages in PDFs, and in simple text format.

It's all about the value of the information they contain, and they can sell for anything from a couple of dollars right up to a hundred dollars or more. Whatever you sell your eBook for, it's all profit.

The most common price point is somewhere between \$5 and \$30. Obviously, the more you sell them for (higher price), the fewer copies you have to sell in order to make your desired income.

You may find out that you'll sell more copies if the price of your book is cheaper, however the more expensive it is, the higher the value of your book and you may actually sell more copies at that higher price! Volume is important though.

The only way to find out what works in your market is to try it and see. And of course to look at the competing offerings out there. Your book might be more expensive but better, or it could be less comprehensive and cheaper — either position is valid.

You will need to setup a website. Perhaps, a blog about your niche to sell your book, and you will also want to promote it on social media, and build a mailing list to sell your book and other products (getting traffic to your website, using social media, and building a mailing list are whole subjects on their own which will be covered separately in my later series of books).

The beauty of this passive income idea is that it is very passive. Once you've written the book and setup your website or other sales channel, it looks after itself. It's also very scalable — you can just produce more books.

A typical eBook might take 3 or 4 days to produce, could you do one per month?

Your book might only earn a few hundred dollar per month, but what if you have ten of them... or 20. eBooks often continue to sell for years after they were originally written, with little or no ongoing work.

To handle the sales process, delivery, and payment, you can either sign up with a service like Gumroad, or implement it in your own website. The Gumroad route is probably much easier, and they also handle all the EU VAT for you, which is a major headache for publishing countries selling eBooks in the EU.

Alternatively, rather than producing your own books or information products, you can also sell works written by others.

This has the advantage of not having to produce the book or product yourself, and you can promote products that are already proven sellers. You promote the product in exactly the way that you would if it was your own, but you send them to the vendor's sales page (probably via an affiliate link, see below), rather than your own sales page.

2. Start a blog with affiliate links

The strategy here is to create content that will attract and engage your audience, and then send them to other sites that will pay you a commission if they buy it. There are many ways to do this.

One is to create a review site for the products you are promoting, so that people will read your reviews, and if they are interested, they go off and buy the product. This is a fairly transparent strategy, and to be honest it's been done to death in recent years. Nevertheless, if you can find a niche that hasn't been over-exploited in this way, then it can still be a winning strategy.

Perhaps a better way, rather than just producing a site full of reviews on products that you're promoting, is to produce a site full of useful and helpful content, that happens to include affiliate links in context.

 For example, you could have a site all about windsurfing that contains useful tips, techniques, tutorials, and interesting articles, and include some affiliate links where appropriate. You could have links to books about windsurfing on Amazon, links to windsurfing gear for sale on Amazon and eBay, links to courses, boards, sails etc, but make these links relevant and in context.

So you're giving useful, helpful information, and mentioning by the way, 'this product happens to be really good for X and if you're looking for Y, then this one is better.'

This type of advice-led promotion is far more useful to your audience than just promoting products for the sake of doing it. You're adding real value through personal recommendation so your audience will appreciate it more. They are also far more likely to buy when they get there.

Affiliate Marketing attracts an awful lot of junk. There are a lot of people promoting spammy offers with low-quality content, blatantly trying to make a fast buck, and usually failing.

The low-quality, spammy approach is so prevalent, you may be tempted to think that it's normal, and consider doing similar things yourself. Don't! You will only harm your reputation and it probably won't work anyway.

My advice is to only promote things you have personal experience with, and don't promote anything that you would not be happy to recommend to your best friend. Never promote anything just to make an affiliate commission, think of helping people first, and getting a commission in return, rather than the other way around.

You can find affiliate offers by joining affiliate networks such as TradeDoubler, Commission Junction, LinkShare, Affiliate Window etc, or by looking for an 'Affiliate Program' section on a merchant's website (often buried in the footer).

Or you can become an affiliate for websites like Amazon or eBay, who sell products in virtually every category under the sun. They also have the advantage of paying you whatever the customer buys, even if it's not the product you were promoting! This can raise your commissions considerably, especially around holiday times when people tend to buy lots of things at once.

It's worth mentioning affiliate marketing for digital products (downloads, eBooks, courses) as these can pay very high commissions, are sometimes well over 50%. The reason for this is that there is no cost of goods sold — a digital product is usually 100% margin, so many publishers will pay their affiliates very high commissions to get more sales.

A significant source of these products, and a massive source of revenue for many affiliates is ClickBank. Clickbank has high-paying digital products available for virtually every niche, and lots of people make enormous money from ClickBank and similar sites like JVZoo.

Beware though, there are lots of low-quality, spammy offers on these sites so don't get involved in anything that doesn't meet your quality standards. Some merchants will give you a free copy of a digital product for review purposes (just ask), still others will require you to buy a copy yourself as proof of your commitment and to make sure you have used the product before you promote it.

3. Make and sell an online course

If you have some skills or knowledge that would be useful to others, then making and selling an online course is a great way to build a passive income. You spend a few hours or days creating your course, which then sells for whatever you like, but typically for somewhere between $20 and $100.

You might need to update your course periodically, but there's no reason why your course couldn't provide income for you several years after you created it.

You can either self-host your course on your own website, which means you have to setup your own course delivery and payment system, or you could host it on a site like Udemy. Udemy is the world's biggest online learning marketplace, with over 10 million students taking courses in everything from programming to yoga and photography.

The advantage of using a platform like Udemy is not just that all your technical issues are taken care of but also it's a marketplace where people go to look for courses like yours. You will get customers that you wouldn't otherwise have gotten, simply by being on Udemy. And if your course is good, and does well, then it will be promoted by Udemy.

Of course, you should still promote your course yourself on your website and other media, but being on a platform that has a ready made following will help you tremendously.

Udemy has a free course that will teach you how to create your first course, and they have a list of hot course topics that they need for more courses. Even if you don't already have the existing skills or knowledge to make a course right off the bat, there's nothing stopping you from finding a suitable topic, researching it and producing a course on it.

4. Build an online drop shipping store

Online stores are an obvious way to make money, and platforms such as Shopify make it very easy to setup and run a very high-quality ecommerce site.

You can now create an online store in a few hours, with all the order processing and payment systems built in. The sort of store that used to cost tens of thousands to build can now be created on Shopify and hosted for a few dollars per month.

But an online store isn't very passive. Once you've made a sale, you then have to pack and ship the goods, and you have to do that in real time as soon as they order, to keep your customers happy. This may disturb your gin and juice time, and doesn't really fit in with our passive income model.

That's where drop shipping comes in. A drop shipper is a manufacturer or distributor who will take your order and ship it directly to your customer on your behalf, thus relieving you of that task. All you have to do is pass the order to your supplier, which can be setup to occur automatically, and they take care of the rest.

You will inevitably have to get involved in some customer service issues, and pre-sales inquiries, and possibly even returns and warranty issues, but these can be dealt with online, or even outsourced to a VA (virtual assistant). You are probably better off doing everything yourself at first, so that you get a good understanding of your customers, and learn your business, but in time most of it can be outsourced to make the income more passive.

The advantages of drop shipping are: firstly you don't have to invest in inventory or stock — you don't buy anything until you have already sold it. Secondly, you can sell anything you like, as long as you can find a supplier who will drop ship it. (just google keyword +"drop shipping" to find suppliers). Two key success factors in drop shipping, are choosing high-value products with a healthy profit on each sale, and finding suppliers who have a MAP (minimum advertised price) policy which preserves your margins.

The best way to find products and suppliers for drop shipping is the SaleHoo Directory.

You can use this to find the most profitable products to sell, and also to find verified suppliers who will drop ship them for you (not just in the USA, but also in UK & Europe).

Their Market Research Lab will help you find products with high sales and low competition, and show you the average selling prices and price trends so you can spot margin opportunities.

Once you've found a product that you want to sell, the next challenge is finding a supplier.

Wholesalers are notoriously bad at promoting themselves, because they are trade-only outlets. People in the trade already know who they are so they don't bother promoting themselves, and often won't even appear on Google.

Their websites can appear shockingly bad, and even amateurish, for the same reason. Even if they are a very reputable wholesaler.

In fact, a polished website that is easy to find, is almost a contra-indication. These wholesalers are only for people in the know — they don't want to attract the public, as they are trade-only suppliers.

There are many scammers claiming to 'wholesale' some of these high-demand products, and often they have the best websites! It can be easy for the unwary to get hoodwinked.

The SaleHoo Directory contains 1.6 million wholesale products from 8000+ genuine wholesale suppliers, all with genuine wholesale prices.

They also have some useful training resources to help you find your way around in this business, and a private forum for buyers and sellers where you can go and ask for help.

This all costs $67, and that lasts for a whole year, which has to be something of a bargain considering the time that it's going to save you in getting started, and the market intelligence it's going to give you.

Check out SaleHoo Directory here.

5. Buy an existing website and improve it

This is not so much of a passive income strategy in and of itself, it's more of an alternative way of implementing one. There are thousands of ready-made websites and blogs for sale, with existing content, traffic, and even proven income streams.

Often, these are for sale because people have lost interest, run out of time, or have moved on to something different.

Some of the sites may have been neglected for a while and need to be brought up to date or they were abandoned part way through and need finishing.

Others may be up to date and ready to go, and some have been created specifically to be sold.

Buying an existing site can save you months of work, especially if it already has traffic, so this can be very worthwhile. You can find websites for sale from a few dollars, right up to hundreds of thousands, depending upon their traffic, name recognition and earnings.

It is probably the quickest way to start an online business — you can start earning within a few hours of buying your site.

In fact, the whole process from not, to having one, to finding a site, buying it, and earning from it, can take as little as 48 hours.

You will of course need some seed money to buy the site, but this does not need to be a huge amount — maybe just one or two hundred dollars. Sites with higher earning potential will naturally be more expensive, but you can choose a site that suits your budget.

The real goal though is to buy a site that is not realizing its potential at the moment, and therefore buy it for less than it's worth.

To do this, you need to know how to appraise the value of a site, and how to increase the earnings once you've bought it.

You also need to know the correct way to carry out due diligence to make sure you're not buying a dud!

The best resource I know that will teach you all these things, is a guide from Yaro Starak, called How to Buy and Sell Blogs & Websites for Passive Profits.

The guide is $49 for a digital copy and instant download, which means you can get started right away.

It will show you exactly where to find blogs to buy (including some places you'd never think to look!), and how to rejuvenate them to increase their earnings and consequently yours.

You can then keep them as a passive income stream, or flip them (sell them) for an instant profit.

6. Sell photographs online

If you have talent with a camera, you can turn it into a passive income source. You can upload your photographs to websites such as Shutterstock, and iStockphoto which provide you with a platform to sell them. You earn with either a percentage or a flat fee for each photo that is sold.

These sites have thousands of people visiting them every day, specifically looking for photographs to buy. Your best chance of success are to specialize in a particular area, which could be a particular location, or a topic such as sailing, business, food, investment, training. As always, do your research carefully, and try to identify gaps in what is currently available. Clip art remains popular online.

You don't have to be the best photographer in the world, just be able to produce good quality, competent photographs of in-demand subjects. These photographs are bought by publishers, editors, writers, bloggers, and other people looking to illustrate or advertise an idea, article, or advert.

The huge growth of social media has increased demand for stock photography massively, particularly for photos with space for people to add text around the image. This is often overlooked by photographers, so if your image allows space for a caption or heading within the image, your photo may get picked over others for that reason.

If you build a good portfolio of photographs, they can generate sales for years to come. You could combine it with your passion, say by taking photographs of your travels or hobby, and selling them so you're truly getting paid for doing something that you love. You could take pictures of the Great Barrier Reef for a dive shop webpage. The results are endless.

7. Fulfillment by Amazon

Fullfillment by Amazon is a service from Amazon that makes it possible to make a passive income by selling physical products. You simply source your products and ship them to Amazon, and they sell and deliver them for you. All you have to do is get your stock to Amazon, and then they take care of everything else, including payment and any customer service or returns issues.

Amazon is much more than just a fulfilment service, it's one of the biggest online marketplaces in the world with thousands of visitors every hour. If you can get your products featured on Amazon, or listed at the top of searches for your category, then you're guaranteed your product is going to be seen by thousands of anxious buyers. There are specific tactics for achieving this, which are covered in the many online courses and articles on Fulfillment By Amazon.

Choosing the right product is obviously important. It needs to be a product that sells in sufficient quantity, with a good margin (the difference between cost price and selling price), and where you can differentiate yourself in some way from the competition.

One method that is quite popular is to create your own brand and repackage other people's products as your own, under your own brand. This is known as white-labeling.

A white label product is a product manufactured by one company and then packaged and sold by other companies under their own brand names. It appears to be a unique product, you can set your own price, and differentiate it from competitors, perhaps by targeting a specific need or application.

Because manufacturing in China is so cheap, it's often possible to find a white-label product in China that you can import and sell for a substantial profit. There is a whole industry that has sprung up around this, and websites like Alibaba specialize in helping you find suppliers in China.

Some of the most mundane products can actually produce quite enormous revenues, simply because of the volume of sales possible on Amazon. You could, for example, earn as much as $100,000 a year selling a meat thermometer — I know someone who does! Giveaway a few of your products when you enter the market in exchange for an online review. Products with favorable reviews differentiate themselves on that alone.

The disadvantage of FBA is that you have to buy your stock up front before you sell it, and if you're going to white-label, you will often have large minimum order quantity to make it worthwhile. However, profit margins are usually big enough to support this — you won't have to sell all your stock to get your original investment back, and once you've done that, all the rest is pure profit.

The secret is to investigate your market and research your product very carefully, find a good supplier and strike a good deal, and then learn how to promote your product within Amazon. There is a lot to learn, and it's probably worth buying one of the online courses to get a head start and increase your chances of success. If you can make it work, you can do very well with an FBA business.

8. Create a membership site

Membership sites are often touted as the ultimate passive income model. A membership site is where you charge a monthly fee for membership which gives people access to exclusive content or services. They offer the promise of a recurring monthly income which increases as you add more members, and if you extrapolate even steady growth, the numbers can look very appealing.

Say you charge $40 per month for access, and you add just 20 members per month, then after a year that equates to 600 per month. However, it doesn't usually work like that.

Most membership sites give access to training materials and resources, which can be very valuable for a few months. After a few months though, most people will have completed all the training and read all the resources, and are unlikely to keep subscribing.

Research shows that the average membership of a site like this is only around three months, so you have to cope with attrition, or loss of subscribers. However, if you can continue adding members quicker than you lose them, or if you can construct a lasting benefit to keep people subscribing then you can still achieve an increasing monthly income.

It's all about creating something of value that is worth the monthly subscription for as long as possible, and continuing to promote it to gain new subscribers. Often, this consists of training materials and other resources that can be created in advance, but you will have to provide fresh content to retain subscribers, or services such as weekly coaching calls, webinars, forums, goal setting, accountability partnerships, mentoring or email support. This makes it not quite so passive, but you can structure this in a way that suits you.

A good way to create an enduring value is to create a community within the membership, either within your website or in something like a Facebook private group. If people receive value from the community, this too will keep them subscribing, although be warned, it is not easy to create communities. And in the early stages you are going to do a lot of work yourself.

A membership site, while it can be very lucrative, is perhaps one of the least passive of the ideas covered here, as it does require a lot of maintenance. However, very few passive income ideas are completely passive, and if you can structure it in a way that suits your desired lifestyle, then it can still be a winner.

The nice thing about a membership site though is by default it creates loyalty because people want their monies worth and will feel like they are getting it the more they use it.

One of the best resources to learn about this business model is from Yaro Starak at Entrepreneur's Journey.

9. Build a Tee Shirt / Merchandise store

You may have seen all the adverts on Facebook for T-shirts with a catchy slogan referencing your name, hobby, or university. Although this has been done a lot over the past couple of years, there is still plenty of room in the market. People will always buy T-shirts, hoodies and other merchandise, particularly if it speaks to an interest or passion of theirs.

The business is very simple. Starting a new tee shirt brand is very inexpensive and quick. Once you've come up with some ideas for designs, you can be up and running in just a few hours. You just need to create an online store in Shopify and connect it to a T - shirt printer/dropshipper through one of their built-in integrations.

Startup costs are very low — almost nothing. A top-flight online store will cost you $29 per month at Shopify (there is a 14 day free trial to get you started for free), and you don't need to buy any stock. The drop shipper handles that, and doesn't print your shirts until you've sold them.

Upload your designs, set your pricing, and the dropshipper will print your designs on demand and ship them straight to your customers.

Produce some designs which will appeal to people with particular interests (e.g. The college they attended, their football team, hobby, name etc) and target these people with Facebook ads and other media. If you don't have the design skills yourself, then you can outsource this on Fiverr or UpWork.

Be creative and come up with something people will always like, and they will buy it. It's then just a question of making sure that your profit on sales exceeds your advertising costs, and you're making money.

The thing to do is to start with very small scale advertising and see what works. You can start advertising on Facebook for as little as $1 per day, and as this is a drop shipping business, you don't actually buy your tee shirts until you've sold them. You're therefore not risking money on designs that might not sell.

Once you find a design and an advert that works well, you simply scale it up and sell more. Ones they are not profitable, you simply drop (unless you can improve them, and make them profitable). It's all about starting small, testing, and then running with your winners.

And of course you don't have to rely solely on paid advertising, you can also promote your designs for free on social media, forums, blogs, newsletters, etc.

Shopify has produced a very comprehensive, step by step guide on exactly how to do it: How To Start An Online T-Shirt Business – the Ultimate Guide. I highly recommend you read, learn and inwardly digest this guide and you will be an expert before you even start.

This business is fairly passive once you have created your designs and setup your ad campaigns. However, designs (and adverts) have a shelf life; so you will have to come up with new designs and adverts to keep the business growing.

10. Write a Kindle book

There have been massive success stories with Kindle books. Because of the size of the Amazon marketplace, and the sheer volume it is capable of delivering. If you get it right, Kindle books can be extremely profitable. And once you've written the book, and established some rankings within Amazon, the book will continue to sell on it's own, maybe for years to come.

Writing a book isn't difficult, and you can always get people to edit it or even help you write it. There are some issues with formatting a book for Kindle, depending on which platform and software you use (eg. Mac or PC), but these are easy to overcome.

The most important thing is researching your book before you write it, to ensure you produce the right book — a book that is going to sell. Get the pulse on the marketplace, what are people reading or currently interested. Google adwords is an excellent tool to find this data.

Once you've produced your book, there are specific ways of marketing it within Amazon, and promoting it, so that it gains some traction in the Amazon marketplace. This process is crucial to the success of your Kindle book so I highly recommend you either take one of the online courses, or read everything you can get your hands on about publishing and marketing Kindle books.

If you can get Amazon to feature or recommend your book, and place it higher in the listings, this will boost your sales enormously. A common way of doing this, is to run a free promotion where people can get the book for free for a limited period, which helps it get noticed and can increase sales once it comes off promotion (also I can tell you it feels pretty good when your book gets to the number one best selling book in it's category, even if it does fall again when it's no longer free!).

Most successful Kindle authors will tell you it's important to have several Kindle books, as people will buy one and often then buy the others. This will multiply your sales. Maybe do a series or trilogy.

Potential earnings are quite significant. If you have a few books, and can sell a few thousand copies per month, typically at around $3 or so. A monthly income of $10,000 is quite achievable, and once you have written the books, this income is completely passive.

If you want to develop passive income from Kindle books, then there is a bit to learn. It's not too hard to do, and there is a step-by-step system that is proven to work, but you do need to learn all this stuff before you get started; otherwise you'll waste hours and your books won't sell as well.

This is the first eBook in a series of eBooks I plan to produce. The remainder of the series will go into detail as to how to implement each passive income technique outlined in this eBook.

Passive income is achievable for anyone who is committed to changing his or her financial situation. Earning passive income puts you at an advantage over other people who are getting their income by working for others. If you desire to own a healthy and wealthy lifestyle, you must not depend on your nine-to-five job. Instead, you want to set-up a passive income stream.

Copyright © **by Brandon K. Gates**

brandon@passivejunkies.com

www.ingramcontent.com/pod-product-compliance
Lightning Source LLC
Chambersburg PA
CBHW081245170526
45165CB00009B/3209